The Ultimate Dropshipping Guide

by Neo Monefa

Table of Contents

21. THANK YOU FOR READING!

1. Introduction

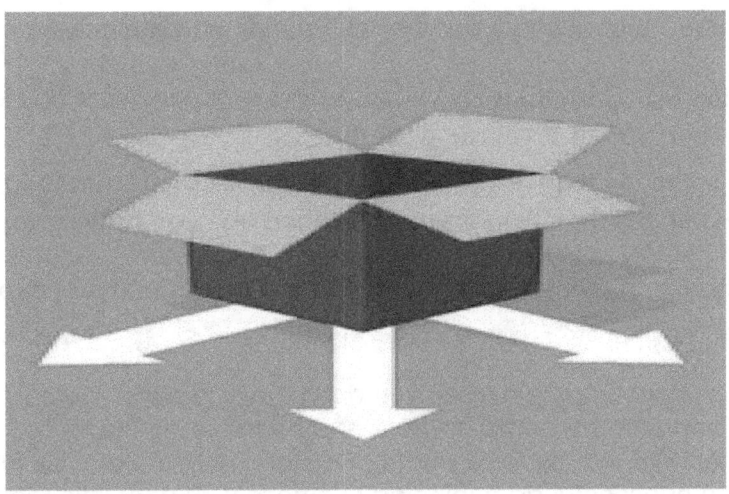

Dropshipping is a retail fulfillment method where a store doesn't keep the products it sells in stock. Instead, when a store sells a product, it purchases the item from a third party and has it shipped directly to the customer. As a result, the merchant never sees or handles the product.

The biggest difference between dropshipping and the standard retail model is that the selling merchant doesn't stock or own inventory. Instead, the merchant purchases inventory as needed from a third party – usually a wholesaler or manufacturer – to fulfill orders.

2. Pros vs Cons

This unique model has a number of benefits and drawbacks:

Benefits

Less Capital Is Required – Probably the biggest advantage to dropshipping is that it's possible to launch an ecommerce store without having to invest thousands of dollars in inventory up front. Traditionally, retailers have had to tie up huge amounts of capital purchasing inventory.

With the dropshipping model, you don't have to purchase a product unless you already made the sale and have been paid by the customer. Without major up-front inventory investments, it's possible to start a successful dropshipping business with very little money.

Easy to Get Started – Running an ecommerce business is much easier when you don't have to deal with physical products. With dropshipping, you don't have to worry about:

Managing or paying for a warehouse
Packing and shipping your orders
Tracking inventory for accounting reasons
Handling returns and inbound shipments
Continually ordering products and managing stock level

Low Overhead – Because you don't have to deal with purchasing inventory or managing a warehouse, your overhead expenses are quite low. In fact, many successful dropshipping businesses are run from a home office with a laptop for less than $100 per month. As you grow, these expenses will likely increase but will still be low compared to those of traditional brick-and-mortar businesses.

Flexible Location – A dropshipping business can be run from just about anywhere with an internet connection. As long as you can communicate with suppliers and customers easily, you can run and manage your business.

Wide Selection of Products – Because you don't have to pre-purchase the items you sell, you can offer an array of products to your potential customers. If suppliers stock an item, you can list if for sale on your website at no additional cost.

Easy to Scale – With a traditional business, if you receive three times as much business you'll usually need to do three times as much work. By leveraging dropshipping suppliers, most of the work to process additional orders will be borne by the suppliers, allowing you to expand with fewer growing pains and less incremental work. Sales growth will always bring additional work – especially related to customer service – but business that utilize dropshipping scale particularly well relative to traditional ecommerce businesses.

All these benefits make dropshipping a very attractive model to both beginning and established merchants. Unfortunately, dropshipping isn't all roses and rainbows. All this convenience and flexibility comes at a price.

Disadvantages

Low Margins – Low margins are the biggest disadvantage to operating in a highly competitive dropshipping niche. Because it's so easy to get started – and the overhead costs are so minimal – many merchants will set up shop and sell items at rock-bottom prices in an attempt to grow revenue. They've invested so little in getting the business started so they can afford to operate on minuscule margins.

True, these merchants often have low-quality websites and poor (if any) customer service. But that won't stop customers from comparing their prices to yours. This increase in cutthroat competition will quickly destroy the profit margin in a niche. Fortunately, you can do a lot to mitigate this problem by selecting a niche that's well suited for dropshipping. We'll discuss this more in Chapter 4.

Inventory Issues – If you stock all your own items, it's relatively simple to keep track of which items are in and out of stock. But when you're sourcing from multiple warehouses, which are also fulfilling orders for other merchants, inventory changes on a daily basis. While there are ways you can better sync your store's inventory with your suppliers', these solutions don't always work seamlessly, and suppliers don't always support the technology required.

Shipping Complexities – If you work with multiple suppliers – as most drop shippers do – the products on your website will be sourced through a number of different drop shippers. This complicates your shipping costs.

Let's say a customer places an order for three items, all of which are available only from separate suppliers. You'll incur three separate shipping charges for sending each item to the customer, but it's probably not wise to pass this charge along to the customer, as they'll think you're grossly overcharging for shipping! And even if you did want to pass these charges along, automating these calculations can be difficult.

Supplier Errors – Have you ever been blamed for something that wasn't your fault, but you had to accept responsibility for the mistake anyway?

Even the best dropshipping suppliers make mistakes fulfilling orders – mistakes for which you have to take responsibility and apologize. And mediocre and low-quality suppliers will cause endless frustration with missing items, botched shipments and low-quality packing, which can damage your business's reputation.

Is It Worth It?

As we initially warned, dropshipping isn't a perfect, stress-free way to build a successful business. The model has some definite advantages but comes with a number of built-in complexities and problems you'll need to be able to address.

We'll be examining these problems – and how to best address them – in future chapters. The good news is that with some careful planning and consideration, most of these problems can be resolved and need not prevent you from building a thriving, profitable dropshipping business.

3. The Supply Chain & Fulfillment Process

Supply chain" is a fancy term describing the path a product takes to go from conception through manufacturing and finally into the hands of a customer. If we were talking with hard-core supplier chain gurus, they'd insist a product's supply chain reaches all the way to the mining of the materials (like oil and rubber) used to manufacture an item. But that's a little intense.

For the purposes of this guide, we don't need to get quite that detailed. You simply need to understand the three most applicable players that make up the dropshipping supply chain: manufacturers, wholesalers and retailers.

So here we go:

Manufacturers – Manufacturers create the product and most do not sell directly to the public. Instead, they sell in bulk to wholesalers and retailers.

Buying directly from the manufacturer is the cheapest way to purchase products for resale, but most have minimum purchase requirements you'll need to meet. You'll also need to stock and then re-ship the products when selling them to customers. For these reasons, it's often easier to buy directly from a wholesaler.

Wholesalers – Wholesalers buy products in bulk from manufacturers, mark them up slightly and then sell them to retailers for resale to the public. If they do have purchasing minimums, they're generally much lower than those required by a manufacturer.

Wholesalers will usually stock products from dozens – if not hundreds – of manufacturers and tend to operate in a specific industry or niche. Most are strictly wholesaler operators, meaning they sell only to retailers and not directly to the general public.

Retailers – A retailer is anyone who sells products directly to the public at a markup. If you run a business that fulfills your orders via dropshipping suppliers, you're a retailer.

Dropshipping Is a Service, Not a Role

You'll notice that "dropshipper" isn't one of the players listed in the supply chain. Why? Because any of the three – manufacturer, wholesaler or retailer – can act as a drop shipper!

If a manufacturer is willing to ship its products directly to your customer, it is "dropshipping" on your behalf. Similarly, a retail merchant can offer to dropship, although its pricing won't be as competitive as a wholesaler's because it isn't buying directly from the manufacturer.

Just because someone claims to be a "dropshipper" does not mean you're getting wholesale pricing. It simply means the company will ship products on your behalf. To get the best pricing, you want to make sure you're working directly with a legitimate wholesaler or manufacturer, a topic we'll be covering in-depth in the next chapter.

4. Dropshipping in Action: The Order Process

Now that you understand the players involved, let's take a look at how a drop shipped order gets processed. To illustrate, we'll follow an order placed with our theoretical store, Phone Outlet, an online merchant that specializes in accessories for smart phones. Phone Outlet dropships all of its products directly from a wholesaler we'll call Wholesale Accessories.

Here's a sample of how the entire ordering process might look:

Step 1 – Customer Places Order With Phone Outlet

Mr. Allen needs a case for his new smartphone and places an order via Phone Outlet's online store. Once the order is approved, a few things happen:

Phone Outlet and Mr. Allen get an email confirmation (likely identical) of the new order that is automatically generated by the store software.

Mr. Allen's payment is captured during the checkout process and will be automatically deposited into Phone Outlet's bank account.

Step 2 – Phone Accessory Outlet Places the Order With Its Supplier

This step is usually as simple as Phone Outlet forwarding the email order confirmation to a sales representative at Wholesale Accessories. Wholesale Accessories has Phone Outlet's credit card on file and will bill it for the wholesale price of the goods, including any shipping or processing fees.

Note: Some sophisticated dropshippers will support automatic XML (a common format for inventory files) order uploading or the ability to place the order manually online, but email is the most common way to place orders with dropshipping suppliers because it's universal and easy to use.

Step 3 – Wholesale Accessories Ships the Order

Assuming the item is in stock and the wholesaler was able to successfully charge Phone Outlet's card, Wholesale Accessories will box up the order and ship it directly to the customer. Though the shipment comes from Wholesale Accessories, Phone Outlet's name and address will appear on the return address label and its logo will appear on the invoice and packing slip. Once the shipment has been finalized, Wholesale Accessories will email an invoice and a tracking number to Phone Outlet.

Note: The turnaround time on dropshipped orders is often faster than you'd think. Most quality suppliers will be able to get an order out the door in a few hours, allowing merchants to advertise same-day shipping even when they are using a dropshipping supplier.

Step 4 – Phone Outlet Alerts the Customer of Shipment

Once the tracking number is received, Phone Outlet will send the tracking information to the customer, likely using an email interface that's built in to the online store interface. With the order shipped, the payment collected and the customer notified, the order and fulfillment process is complete. Phone Outlet's profit (or loss) is the difference between what it charged Mr. Allen and what it paid Wholesale Accessories.

5. How to Spot Fake Wholesalers

Depending on where you're searching, you'll likely come across a large number of "fake" wholesalers. Unfortunately legitimate wholesalers are traditionally poor at marketing and tend to be harder to find. This results in the non-genuine wholesalers – usually just middle men – appearing more frequently in your searches, so you'll want to be cautious.

The following tactics will help you discern whether a wholesale supplier is legitimate:

They Want Ongoing Fees – Real wholesalers don't charge their customers a monthly fee for the privilege of doing business and ordering from them. If a supplier asks for a monthly membership or service fee, it's likely not legitimate.

It's important to differentiate here between suppliers and supplier directories. Supplier directories (which we'll discuss shortly) are directories of wholesale suppliers organized by product types or market and screened to ensure the suppliers are legitimate. Most directories will charge a fee – either one time or ongoing – so you shouldn't take this as a sign the directory itself is illegitimate.

They Sell to the Public – To get genuine wholesale pricing you'll need to apply for a wholesale account, prove you're a legitimate business and be approved before placing your first order. Any wholesale supplier that offers products to the general public at "wholesale prices" is just a retailer offering items at inflated prices.

But here are some legitimate dropshipping fees you'll likely encounter:

Per-Order Fees – Many dropshippers will charge a per-order drop hipping fee that can range from $2 to $5 or more, depending on the size and complexity of the items being shipped. This is standard in the industry, as the costs of packing and shipping individual orders are much higher than shipping a bulk order.

Minimum Order Sizes – Some wholesalers will have a minimum initial order size, which is the lowest amount you have to purchase for your first order. They do this in order to filter out window-shopping merchants that will waste their time with questions and small orders but won't translate into meaningful business.

If you're dropshipping, this could cause some complications. For example, what do you do if a supplier has a $500 minimum order, but your average order size is around $100? You don't want to pre-order $500 of product just for the privilege of opening a dropshipping account.

In this situation, it's best to offer to pre-pay the supplier $500 to build a credit with them to apply against your drop shipping orders. This allows you to meet the supplier's minimum purchase requirement (as you're committing to buy at least $500 in product) without having to place a single large order without any corresponding customer orders.

6. Finding Wholesale Suppliers

Now that you can spot a fraud from the real deal, it's time to start searching for suppliers! You can use a number of different strategies, some more effective than others. The methods below are listed in order of effectiveness and preference, with our favorite methods listed first:

Contact the Manufacturer
This is our favorite way to easily locate legitimate wholesale suppliers. If you know the product(s) you want to sell, call the manufacturer and ask for a list of its wholesale distributors. You can then contact these wholesalers to see if they dropship and inquire about setting up an account.

Since most wholesalers carry products from a variety of manufacturers, this strategy will allow you to quickly source a selection of products within the niche you're exploring. After making a couple of calls to the leading manufacturers in a niche, you'll quickly be able to identify the leading wholesalers in that market.

Search Using Google
Using Google to find high-quality suppliers may seem obvious, but there are a few rules to keep in mind:

You Have to Search Extensively – Wholesalers are terrible at marketing and promotion, and they're definitely not going to top the search results for "wholesale suppliers for product X." This means you'll likely have to dig through LOTS of search results – possibly hundreds – to find the wholesaler's website listed way down at #65.

Don't Judge by the Website – Wholesalers are also notorious for having poorly designed '90s-style websites. So while a quality site may indicate a good supplier in some cases, many legitimate wholesalers have cringe-worthy homepages. Don't let the poor design scare you off.

Use Lots of Modifiers – Wholesalers aren't doing extensive SEO to ensure you find their websites, so you might need to try various search queries. Don't stop at just "[product] wholesaler." Try using modifiers such as "distributor," "reseller," "bulk," "warehouse" and "supplier."

Order From the Competition

If you're having a hard time locating a supplier, you can always use the old order-from-the-competition trick. Here's how it works: Find a competitor you think is dropshipping and place a small order with that company. When you receive the package, Google the return address to find out who the original shipper was. In some cases, it will be a supplier you can contact.

This is a tactic we've heard discussed by others but haven't used ourselves. And if you haven't been able to find a supplier using the other techniques discussed above, there might be a good reason (i.e., the market is too small, there's not enough demand to justify a supplier, etc.). So keep this technique in mind, but don't rely too heavily on it.

Attend a Trade Show

A trade show allows you to connect with all the major manufacturers and wholesalers in a niche. It's a great way to make contacts and research your products and suppliers all in one spot. This only works if you've already selected your niche and/or product, and it isn't feasible for everyone. But if you have the time and money to attend, it's a great way to get to know the manufactures and suppliers in a market.

Directories

One of the most common questions aspiring ecommerce entrepreneurs ask is: Should I pay for a supplier directory?

A supplier directory is a database of suppliers that's organized by market, niche or product. Many directories employ some sort of screening process to ensure the suppliers listed are genuine wholesalers. Most are run by for-profit companies who charge a fee for access to their directory.

While membership directories can be helpful, especially for brainstorming ideas, they are by no means necessary. If you already know the product or niche you want to sell, you should be able to find the major suppliers in your market with a bit of digging and the techniques discussed above. Plus, once you start your business you likely won't need to revisit the directory unless you need to find suppliers for other products.

That said, supplier directories are a convenient way to quickly search for and/or browse a large number of suppliers in one place and are great for brainstorming ideas for products to sell or niches to enter. If you're short on time and are willing to spend the money, they can be a helpful tool.

There are a number of different supplier directories, and a comprehensive review of all of them is beyond the scope of this guide. Instead, we've highlighted some of the most well-known supplier directories online. Please note we are not endorsing any of these directories, we're simply providing you with some options.

Worldwide Brands
Quick Stats:

Established 1999
Thousands of wholesalers
Over 10 million products
Price: $299 for a lifetime membership
Worldwide Brands is one of the oldest and best-known supplier directories. It advertises that it only includes suppliers that meet a set of guidelines to ensure legitimate, quality wholesalers.

We've used the directory in the past to find legitimate wholesalers and to brainstorm niche ideas – and found it useful. Though the directory is missing some suppliers we've worked with, it does include a large collection of legitimate wholesalers. If you want lifetime access to a quality directory and are comfortable with a larger one-time payment, Worldwide Brands is a safe bet.

SaleHoo

Quick Stats:

Established 2005
Over 8,000 suppliers
Price: $67 per year
The SaleHoo supplier directory lists more than 8,000 bulk-purchase and dropshipping suppliers, and seems to cater heavily to merchants on eBay, and Amazon.

Although we've never used SaleHoo to source products, its $67 annual price is one of the most compelling values among supplier directories and includes a 60-day money-back guarantee. If you're comfortable paying an annual membership – or only need to use a directory temporarily - SaleHoo might be worth a look.

Doba
Quick Stats:

Established 2002
165 suppliers
Over 1.5 million products
Price: $60 per month
Instead of simply listing suppliers, Doba's service integrates with dropshippers (hence why they only have 165 suppliers) allowing you to place orders with multiple warehouses using its centralized interface. Membership also includes a Push-to-Marketplace tool that automates the process of listing items on eBay.

Doba's centralized system offers more convenience then the other directories which is why we imagine the $60 / month fee is significantly higher than other prices. If you place a high value on convenience and can find the products you want among their suppliers, Doba's interface may be worth the cost.

However, if you can identify quality suppliers on your own and don't mind working with them directly, you'll be able to save around $700 / year. If there are only a few key suppliers in your niche – reducing the number of parties you have to coordinate with – this may be the way to go.

Wholesale Central
Quick Stats:

Established 1996
1,400 suppliers
740,000 products
Price: free
Unlike many other directories, there's no charge to search
Wholesale Central for suppliers because it charges suppliers a fee
to be listed and also displays ads on their site. They also claim to
review and screen all suppliers to ensure they are legitimate and
trustworthy.

It's difficult to argue with free, and there's no harm in browsing the
listings at Wholesale Central, but you'll need to be a bit more
discriminating. A number of the suppliers we found appeared to be

retailers selling to the public at "wholesale" prices – not something a
supplier would do when offering real wholesale pricing. So while
we're sure there are genuine wholesale opportunities listed, you
may want to be a little more thorough with your due diligence.

7. Before You Contact Suppliers

Alright, so you've found a number of solid suppliers and are ready to move forward – great! But before you start contacting companies, you'll want to have all your ducks in a row.

You Need to Be Legal – As we mentioned earlier, most legitimate wholesalers will require proof that you're a legal business before allowing you to apply for an account. Most wholesalers only reveal their pricing to approved customers, so you'll need to be legally incorporated before you'll get to see the kind of pricing you'll receive.

Bottom line? Make sure you're legally incorporated before contacting suppliers! If you're only looking to ask a few basic questions ("Do you drop ship?" "Do you carry brand X?"), you won't need to provide any documentation. But don't expect to launch without having your business properly set up. We'll talk more about setting up your business in Chapter 5.

Understand How You Appear – Wholesalers are constantly bombarded by people with "great business plans" who pepper them with questions, take up a lot time and then never order anything. So if you're launching a new business, be aware that many suppliers aren't going to go out of their way to help you get started.

Most will be happy to set you up with a dropshipping account if they offer it. But don't ask for discount pricing or spend hours tying up their sales representatives on the phone before you've made a single sale. It will quickly earn you a bad reputation and hurt your relationship with the supplier.

If you do need to make special requests (say, trying to convince a supplier to dropship when it normally doesn't), you need to build credibility. Be definitive about your business plans ("We ARE launching this site on January 20) instead of using flaky rhetoric ("I'm thinking about maybe launching a business sometime soon"). And be sure to communicate any professional successes you've had in the past – especially with sales and marketing – that will help you with your new venture.

You need to convince suppliers that the inconvenience of accommodating your special request(s) will pay off down the road when you become successful and start bringing them a ton of business.

Don't Be Afraid of the Phone – One of the biggest fears people have when it comes to suppliers is simply picking up the phone and making the call. For many, this is a paralyzing prospect. You might be able to send emails for some issues, but more often than not you'll need to pick up the phone to get the information you need.

The good news is that it's not as scary as you might think. Suppliers are accustomed to having people call them, including newbie entrepreneurs. You're likely to get someone who's friendly and more than happy to answer your questions. Here's a tip that will help you, simply write out your questions ahead of time. It's amazing how much easier it is to make the call when you've got a list of pre-written questions to ask.

8. How to Find Good Suppliers

Like most things in life, suppliers are not all created equally. In the world of dropshipping – where the supplier is such a critical part of your fulfillment process – it's even more important to make sure you're working with top-notch players.

Great suppliers tend to have many of the following 6 attributes:

Expert Staff and Industry Focus – Top-notch suppliers have knowledgeable sales representatives who really know the industry and their product lines. Being able to call a representative with questions is invaluable, especially if you're launching a store in a niche you're not overly familiar with.

Dedicated Support Representatives – Quality dropshippers should assign you an individual sales representative responsible for taking care of you and any issues you have. We've dealt with wholesalers that don't assign specific representatives and we hate it. Problems take a lot longer to resolve, and we usually have to nag people to take care of an issue. Having a single supplier contact who's responsible for solving your issues is really important.

Invested in Technology – While there are plenty of good suppliers with outdated websites, a supplier that understands the benefits of – and invests heavily in – technology is usually a pleasure to work with. Features such as real-time inventory, a comprehensive online catalog, customizable data feeds and an online searchable order history are pure luxury for online merchants and can help you streamline your operations.

Can Take Orders via Email – This may sound like a minor issue, but having to call every order in – or manually place it on the website – makes processing orders significantly more time-intensive.

Centrally Located – If you're in a large country like the United States, it's beneficial to use a centrally located dropshipper, as packages can reach more than 90% of the country within 2 to 3 business days. When a supplier is located on one of the coasts, it can take more than a week for orders to be shipped across the country. Centrally located suppliers allow you to consistently promise faster delivery times, potentially saving you money on shipping fees.

Organized and Efficient – Some suppliers have competent staff and great systems that result in efficient and mostly error-free fulfillment. Others will botch every fourth order and make you want to tear your hair out. The trouble is, it's difficult to know how competent a supplier is without actually using it.

Although it won't give you a complete picture, placing a few small test orders can give you a great sense of how a supplier operates. You can see:

How they handle the order process
How quickly the items ship out
How rapidly they follow up with tracking information and an invoice
The quality of the pack job when the item arrives
Your Options on Paying Suppliers

The vast majority of suppliers will accept payment in one of two ways:

Credit Card
When you're starting out, most suppliers will require you to pay by credit card. Once you've established a thriving business, paying with credit cards is often still the best option. They're not only convenient (no need to write checks regularly), but you can rack up a LOT of rewards points/frequent flier miles. Because you're buying a product for a customer who has already paid for it on your website, you can rack up a high volume of purchases through your credit card without having to incur any actual out-of-pocket expenses.

Net Terms

The other common way to pay suppliers is with "net terms" on invoice. This simply means that you have a certain number of days to pay the supplier for the goods you've purchased. So if you're on "net 30" terms, you have 30 days from the date of purchase to pay your supplier – by check or bank draw – for the goods you bought.

Usually, a supplier will make you provide credit references before offering net payment terms because it's effectively lending you money. This is a common practice, so don't be alarmed if you have to provide some documentation when paying on net terms.

The biggest hurdle most new dropshipping entrepreneurs face is picking a niche and products to focus on. And it's understandable – it's likely the biggest decision you'll make and has long-term consequences on the success or failure of the business.

The most common mistake at this stage is picking a product based on personal interest or passion. This is an acceptable strategy if being interested in the product is your primary objective, not necessarily business success. But if your #1 goal is to build a profitable dropshipping site, you'll want to consider setting your personal passions aside when doing market research.

9. How to Be Successful Selling Online

To build a successful ecommerce business, you'll need to do one of the following:

Manufacture Your Own Product – You control distribution and are the sole source for the item. This limits competition and allows you to charge a premium price. If you intend to dropship products, you'll be selling existing products manufactured by someone else, so this isn't an option.

Have Access to Exclusive Pricing or Distribution – If you can arrange an exclusive agreement to carry a product – or if you have access to exclusive pricing from a manufacturer – you can profitably sell online without creating your own product. These arrangements can be difficult to arrange, however, and hundreds of other dropship merchants will have access to similar goods and wholesale prices.

Sell at the Lowest Price – If you can offer the lowest price, you'll likely steal business from a large chunk of the market. The only problem? It's a business model doomed to failure. If the only thing of value you have to offer is a low price, you'll be caught in a pricing war that will strip virtually all your profits. Trying to compete against Amazon and other established online giants on price is generally a poor strategy.

Add Value in Non-Pricing Terms – Offering valuable information that complements your products is the BEST way to differentiate yourself and charge a premium price. Entrepreneurs set out to solve people's problems, and that's no different in the world of ecommerce and dropshipping. Offering expert advice and guidance within your niche is the best way to build a profitable dropshipping business.

Adding Value in Ecommerce – Just add value! Simple enough, right? Well, that's easier said than done. Some products and niches lend themselves to this strategy more than others. You should look for a few key characteristics that make adding value with educational content much easier. Specially, you'll want to look for niches that:

Have Many Components – The more components a product needs to function properly, the more likely customers are to turn to the internet for answers. Which purchase is more confusing: buying a new office chair or buying a home security camera system that requires multiple cameras, complex wiring and a recorder?

The more components a product needs – and the more variety among those components – the greater your opportunity to add value by advising customers on which products are compatible.

Are Customizable/Confusing – Along the same vein, confusing and customizable products are perfect for adding value through content. Would you inherently know how to select the best hot water solar panel configuration for your climate or which type of wireless dog collar system is right for your yard? Being able to offer specific guidance on what types of products are best suited for specific environments and customers is a great way to add value.

Require Technical Setup or Installation – It's easy to offer expert guidance for products that are difficult to set up, install or assemble. Take the security camera system from before. Let's say the camera site had a detailed 50-page installation guide that also covered the most common mistakes people make installing their own systems. If you thought the guide could save you time and hassle, there's a good chance you'd buy it from that website even if it was available for a few dollars less elsewhere. For store owners, the guides add tremendous value to customers and don't cost anything to provide once they're created.

Ways to Add Value:

You can add value to complex and confusing niches in a number of ways, including:

Creating comprehensive buyers' guides
Investing in detailed product descriptions and listings
Creating installation and setup guides (as discussed above)
Creating in-depth videos showing how the product works
Establishing an easy-to-follow system for understanding component compatibility
Cherry-Picking the Best Customers

All customers aren't created equally. It's strange how some customers buying small items feel entitled to demand the moon while other big spenders rarely ask for anything.

Targeting the right demographic can be a big boon for your business. These clients tend to make it worth your while:

Hobbyists – People love their hobbies and will spend mind-boggling amounts on equipment, training and tools for them. Many serious mountain bikers have bikes that cost more than their cars, and folks who love to fish might spend a fortune outfitting their boats. If you can target the right hobbyist niche and successfully connect with enthusiasts and their needs, you can do very well.

Businesses – Business clients are sometimes more price-sensitive but will almost always order in larger quantities than individual consumers. Once you've established a rapport and earned their trust, you open the door to a long-term, high-volume profitable relationship. If at all possible, try to sell products that appeal to both individual customers and businesses.

Repeat Buyers – Recurring revenue is a beautiful thing. If you sell products that are disposable and/or need to be reordered frequently, you can grow rapidly as you build a loyal customer base that frequently returns to purchase.

Other Considerations When Selecting Products

The Perfect Price – Make sure you strongly consider the price point relative to the level of pre-sale service you'll need to provide. Most people feel comfortable placing a $200 order online without talking to someone on the phone. But what about a $1,500 item they're unfamiliar with? Chances are, most would want to chat directly with a sales representative before making such a large purchase, both to ensure the item is a good fit and to make sure the store is legitimate.

If you plan to sell high-priced items, make sure you're able to offer personalized phone support. You'll also want to ensure that the margins are rich enough to justify the pre-sale support you'll need to offer. Often, the $50 to $200 price range is the sweet spot to maximize revenue without having to provide extensive pre-sale support.

MAP Pricing – Some manufacturers will set what's called a minimum advertised price (MAP) for their products, and require that all resellers price their products at or above certain levels. This pricing floor prevents the price wars that often break out – especially for products that are easily drop shipped – and helps ensure that merchants can make a reasonable profit by carrying a manufacturer's products.

If you can find a niche where manufacturers enforce MAP pricing it's a huge benefit, especially if you plan on building a high-value and information-rich site. With prices the same across all competitors, you can compete on the strength of your website and won't have to worry about losing business to less reputable but cheaper competition.

Marketing Potential – The time to think about how you'll market a business is before you launch it, not three months in when you realize that customer acquisition is a nightmare. Can you brainstorm a number of ways you could promote your store by, for example, writing articles, giving away products or reaching out to active online communities that use the products you're selling? If not, you may want to reconsider.

Selling a product with many accessories is a great way to improve your overall margin.

Lots of Accessories – As a general rule of retail, margins on lower priced accessories are significantly higher than those of high-priced items. While a cell phone store may only make a 5% margin on the latest smartphone, they'll almost certainly make a 100% or 200% margin on the case that goes with it.

As customers, we're also much more sensitive about the price on a big-ticket item and care less about the price of smaller accessories. To use the previous example, you'd likely shop around for the best price on an expensive smartphone. But are you going to call around to find the best price on a $20 to $30 case? Probably not. You'll likely purchase it from the same store where you bought the phone.

Low Turnover – We hope you're convinced by now that investing in an education-rich, high-quality site will pay big dividends. But if the products you sell change every year, maintaining that site is quickly going to turn into a mountain of work. Try to find products that aren't updated with new models every year. That way, the time and money you invest in a superb site will last longer.

Hard to Find Locally – Selling a product that's hard to find locally will increase your chances of success as long as you don't get too specific. Most people needing a garden rake or a sprinkler would simply run down to the local hardware store. But where would you buy a medieval knight's costume or falcon training equipment? You'd probably head to Google and start searching.

Smaller Is Usually Better – In a world where free shipping is often expected, it can be a challenge to sell large, heavy equipment that's expensive to ship. The smaller the items, the easier they are to ship cheaply to your customers.

Picking a profitable niche isn't easy and requires you to consider numerous factors. These guidelines should give you a good idea of the types of drop shipped products that work well. For more on these attributes, please see this extended article on picking a profitable dropshipping niche.

10. Measuring Demand

Without demand, it doesn't matter if your niche fits 100% of the attributes listed above. If nobody wants your product, you'll have a hard time making any money! As the old saying goes, it's much easier to fill existing demand than to try to create it.

Fortunately, a number of online tools allow you to measure demand for a product or market. The most well-known and popular is the Google Keyword Tool.

Google Keyword Tool

The best way to measure demand for an item online is to see how many people are searching for it using a search engine like Google. Fortunately, Google makes this search volume publicly available via its keyword tool. Simply type in a word or phrase, and the tool tells you how many people are searching for it every month.

There are entire training modules dedicated to using the keyword tool, and we're not able to cover the tool exhaustively in this resource. But keep the following three tips in mind, and you'll be well on your way to getting the most out of the tool:

Match Type – The tool will let you select broad, phrase or exact match types when it reports search volumes. Unless you have a good reason to do otherwise, you should use the exact match option. This will give you a much more accurate picture of the applicable search volume for the keyword. For a more detailed explanation, see this article on understanding match types.

Search Location – Make sure you look at the difference between local search volume (in your country or a user-defined region) and global search volumes. If you'll be selling primarily in the U.S., you should focus on the local search volumes and ignore the global results, as that's where most of your customers will be.

Long-Tail Variations – It's easy to fixate on the broad, one- or two-word search terms that get massive amounts of search volume. In reality, it's the longer, more specific and lower volume search queries that will make up most of your traffic from the search engines. These longer, more detailed search terms are commonly referred to as "long-tail" searches.

Keep this in mind when you're looking at potential markets and niches to enter. If a search term has many variations that are actively searched for, that's a good sign that the market is fairly deep with lots of variety and interest. But if search queries and related volume drop off precipitously after the first few high-level words, there's probably less related long-tail traffic.

To learn more about estimating traffic, see these guides to estimating long-tail traffic and spotting niches with significant long-tail potential.

Google Trends

The keyword tool is great for raw search figures, but for more detailed insights you'll want to use Google Trends. The tool offers you information that the Keyword Tool just doesn't provide, including:

Search Volume Over Time: Ideally, you want the niche you're entering to be growing and Trends can let you know if this is the case. For any given search query, you can see the growth or decline in search volume over time. Below is a chart of search volume for the term "smartphone". As expected, search volume has risen sharply in the last few years:

Top and Rising Terms: You'll also be able to get a snapshot at the most popular related searches, and which queries have been growing in popularity the fastest. Focusing on these popular and quickly growing terms can be helpful when planning your marketing and SEO efforts. According to the charts below, search queries related to AT&T, Verizon and Samsung seem to be experiencing the most growth in the smart phone market – data which shows up when we analyze the term "smartphone":

11. Measuring Competition

Conducting competitive analysis on a potential market can be tricky. Too much competition and you'll have difficulty building traffic and competing with established players. Too little competition can indicate a tiny market that will drastically limit how big you'll be able to grow.

Some dropshipping stores use paid advertising, but most will rely heavily on free traffic from the search engines to build a profitable business model. With this in mind, the best way to measure the overall competition in a market is to examine the organically listed (i.e., not advertised) sites on the first page of Google for a specific term. In order to generate a decent level of traffic, you'll need to successfully compete with (i.e., outrank) the sites on Google's first page.

The world of search engine optimization (SEO) is one we can't do justice in this dropshipping guide. For a more detailed discussion, we highly recommend SEOmoz's comprehensive "Beginner's Guide to SEO" or this more focused 15-minute SEO guide. But for the sake of evaluating competition, these four metrics will help you quickly gauge how strong the field is – and how hard it will be to outrank your competitors and generate traffic.

Number of Linking Domains

Google's ranking algorithm relies heavily on links. All else equal, the more links a site receives the higher it will rank in the search results. Knowing how many links are pointing to a site will give you an idea of how much work you'll need to do (in terms of earning and building links to your own site) to outrank your competitor.

There are dozens of different SEO metrics that are commonly used, but one in particularly is useful when evaluating the ranking strength of a site: the number of unique domains that link to it. Often called "linking root domains" or "unique linking domains", this metric represents the number of unique domains (ie independent sources) that link to a site and ignores duplicate links from the same domain.

To best understand this concept it's helpful to think of links like personal recommendations. If your best friend comes to you and recommends a restaurant, you may remember it. And if he raves about it every day for a week (a total of seven recommendations) you'll likely be moved to eat there. But even his fanaticism wouldn't be nearly as powerful as if seven unique, unrelated friends highly recommended the restaurant. Because they're independent sources, their recommendations hold much more authority.

The same is true when analyzing links to a site. A domain can link to a site repeatedly, but it's really one "unique" recommendation, and this is where common SEO metrics like "total number of links" can paint an inaccurate picture when measuring a site's strength. Instead, looking at the number of unique linking domains will give you a much better idea of how difficult it will be to compete with a site in the search results. Google places a high emphasis on unique linking domains, so you should, too.

The best way to get this figure is to use a tool called Open Site Explorer. Developed by a company called SEOMoz, Open Site Explorer provides a number of valuable SEO metrics and data. For full functionality, you'll need to purchase a paid membership but it's possible to get the metric we want - "Linking Root Domains" as labeled by the tool – for free.

When examining Google's search results, you'll want to look most carefully at the link metrics for the top few sites (#1 and #2 in Google) as well as the link metrics for the last site on the front page (#10 in Google). This will give you a rough idea of how much work is needed to not only rank #1, but also to simply make it on the first page of search results. The vast majority of searchers ends up clicking on one of the top ten results in Google, so you want to understand how difficult it will be to get your site ranked there.

Here's a quick cheat sheet for interpreting the number of unique linking domains. (These are only rough guidelines but should help you make sense of the numbers.)

0 to 50 Linking Root Domains: Will likely be on the low end for most worthwhile markets. Most sites with quality content and some focused marketing and SEO effort should be able to get 50 linking domains within a year.

50 to 250 Linking Root Domains: This is a more realistic range for top-ranked sites in decently sized niche markets. It may take a multi-year approach to build a backlink profile in this range, but it's feasible. A competitive landscape with this profile often offers the best work-to-reward ratio, especially for individual dropshipping entrepreneurs or very small teams.

250+ Linking Root Domains: Unless you're a talented marketer or SEO ninja, building up more than 250 unique links will take some serious time and commitment. It's not always a deal killer – just make sure you're ready to face some entrenched competition.

Authority of Competing Sites

When determining a site's rank, Google doesn't just look at the number of links a site has. It also considers the quality of those links. So a link from Mike's Marshmallow Blog with five readers won't count anywhere close to as much as a link from The New York Times.

The metric Google uses to measure a page's authority is called PageRank. It's not the end-all-be-all of SEO metrics, but it's a quick way to get an idea of how important Google thinks a page is. As with unique linking sites, you can get a sense for how competitive a market is by looking at the PageRank for the homepages of top-ranked sites.

The easiest way to check PageRank is with a browser extension such as SearchStatus for Firefox. You can also check sites manually using sites like this one.

Here's a quick way to interpret PageRank readings for a site's homepage:

PageRank 1 to 2: A relatively small amount of authority. PageRank in this range for the top homepages likely indicates a relatively small market.

PageRank 3 to 4: A much more common range for highly ranked sites in competitive niche markets. It's not necessarily easy to reach this level of authority – but not impossible, either. Markets in this range usually offer the best work-to-reward range for individual drop shippers.

PageRank 4 to 5: A fairly high level of authority. To reach this level, you'll need to get numerous links from respected, authoritative sites, in addition to a fair number of other links.

PageRank 6+: You've got a full-time marketing and SEO department, right? Because you'll need them to compete in a market with sites like this.

Qualitative Metrics to Consider

Hard statistics like unique linking domains and PageRank can be helpful in determining how hard it will be to outrank competitors, but it's also very important to look at a few qualitative factors:

Site Quality and Usefulness – Visit the top-ranked sites for a market and put yourself in the shoes of a customer. Do they appear inviting and welcoming or old and outdated? Are the sites well-organized and easy to navigate or is it a struggle to even find the search box? Do they provide high-quality information and detailed product listings or do you have to squint to make out the grainy product images?

In short, how likely would you be to purchase from those sites? If you're blown away by the top sites in a market, it will be difficult to differentiate yourself and you may want to consider a different market. But if there's a lot of room for improvement – or, as we see it, opportunity to add value – that's a great sign.

Site Reputation and Customer Loyalty – An online business might have a solid reputation based on years of treating customers well, despite a drab design and outdated site. Alternatively, the most beautifully designed site might have a widespread reputation for awful customer service. It can be difficult to judge a book by its cover.

Check with the Better Business Bureau to see if a company has a history of customer complaints. You'll also want to do a web search to see what people are saying on social media and in online forums and communities. If the top competitors are slacking in the service and satisfaction department, there might be an opening for a store with superior service.

An Important Note on
Search Results

When you perform a search, it's important to realize that Google personalizes the results you see based on your geographic location, your browsing history and other factors. When we're analyzing a market, we need to see unbiased results so we can understand the real competitive landscape. Also, if you're living outside the states but plan on selling to US customers you need access to the search results your US-based customers will see as those are the sites you'll be competing with.

There are two ways to get around these issues:

Incognito Search: If you use Chrome as a browser, you can browse the web 'Incognito'. In this mode, any personalized settings or browsing history will discarded so you can get an unbiased idea of how sites actually rank. You can start an Incognito browsing sessions by going to "File → New Incognito Window" or by clicking on the icon in the upper right hand corner of your browser and selecting "New Incognito Window". Other web browsers have similar 'hidden search' modes that will clear your browsing history.

Forcing Nation-Specific Results: If you'd like to see the results that appear for a nation other than your own, you can add a small amount of text to the end of the URL on a Google results page to get country specific results.

For a more detailed explanation of how to implement this, please see this guide to tweaking geo-targeting with Google and this list of country codes used by Google.

12. Deciding on a Business Structure

If you're serious about your venture, you'll want to set up a legitimate business entity. We're not lawyers and can't offer legal advice but we can give you a rundown of three commonly used business structures:

Sole Proprietorship – This is the simplest business structure to implement but also offers no personal liability protection. So if your business is sued, your personal assets also may be in jeopardy. Filing requirements are minimal, and you simply report your business's earnings on your personal taxes. No other state or federal business filings are required.

Limited Liability Company (LLC) – An LLC offers increased protection of your personal assets by establishing your business as a separate legal entity. While the liability protection isn't foolproof, it does offer more protection than a sole proprietorship. You may need to comply with additional filing requirements and will need to pay both incorporation and ongoing fees.

C Corporation – Most major corporations are set up as C corporations which, when done properly, offer the most liability protection. They are likely to be more expensive to incorporate and are subject to double taxation, as income doesn't pass directly to the shareholders.

So which structure to choose? Again, we're not lawyers and would advise you to consult with one before making any incorporation decisions. Most small entrepreneurs tend to go with either a sole proprietorship or an LLC. Personally, we've used an LLC for all of our dropshipping businesses because we feel it offers the best trade-off regarding liability protection, autonomy from personal finances and costs.

Requesting an EIN Number

The IRS requires all businesses to have an employer identification number (EIN), which acts as a Social Security number for your business. You'll need this number to file your taxes, apply for wholesale dropshipping accounts, open a bank account and pretty much do anything related to your business.

Fortunately, getting an EIN number is easy and free. You can easily apply for an EIN number online.

Getting Your Finances in Order

One common mistake entrepreneurs make when starting a business is blending their personal and business finances. This causes confusion, makes accounting more difficult, can lead to personal assumption of business liabilities and is a big red flag for the IRS if you're ever audited.

You'll want to keep your business and personal finances separate as much as possible. The best way to do that is by opening up new accounts in your business's name. You'll want to open a new:

Business Checking Account – You should run all of your business finances through one primary checking account. All business revenue should be deposited into it and all expenses should be withdrawn from it. This will make accounting much easier and cleaner.

PayPal Account – If you plan to accept PayPal (which you likely will), you'll want a separate account for your business.

Credit Card – You should have a business credit card that is used for business expenses and dropshipping inventory purchases only. Because you'll be buying a lot of merchandise from suppliers, you can rack up some serious rewards with the right rewards travel cards. We've found that Capital One has the best travel rewards program, and that Fidelity Visa/American Express offers the best cash-back program.

Collecting Sales Tax

You'll need to collect sales tax only if both the following are true:

The state you operate from collects sales tax AND
An order is placed by someone living in your state
For all orders placed by residents of other states – even if those

states charge their own sales tax – you won't need to collect any tax. There's a good chance we'll see changes to these laws in the coming years, but for now the tax laws for small online merchants are very advantageous.

If your state does charge sales tax, be prepared to collect it on the limited number of orders from customers in your home state. You'll want to contact your state's Department of Commerce to register as a retailer and find out how frequently you need to submit the tax you collect.

Local Business Licenses

Most cities and towns require businesses to get a business license that needs to be renewed on a regular basis. However, this requirement may differ for dropshipping businesses, many of which will likely be operated from home offices. You'll want to look into your local laws and regulations to see what, if anything, is required.

Incorporating Outside the U.S.

It can be complex, but it's possible for international merchants to incorporate a business in the United States, giving them access to U.S. based dropshippers and customers. The merchant will need to come to the U.S. to complete the necessary paperwork, have a trusted business partner in the U.S. who can act on his behalf or hire an agency to set everything up.

Evaluating Sales Channels

With a product picked, suppliers secured and your business legally established, it's time to start selling! Next, you need to decide how to get your products in front of prospective customers. Several sales options are available, but you'll most likely choose one or a combination of selling on your own online store, eBay, or Amazon.

13. Dropshipping on eBay

As the world's largest auction site for physical goods online, eBay is a site most people know well. The following are some reasons you might want to consider – or avoid – dropshipping on eBay:

The Pros of Selling on eBay

Easy to Get Started – With eBay you can immediately dive in and start listing your wholesale products. Create an account, add a listing and you're in business.

Access to a Large Audience – When you list on eBay, you have access to the many online buyers who frequent the auction giant. Millions of people will see your listings, and the fairly robust and active market will help ensure you get a decent price for your products.

Less Marketing – Because you're able to piggyback off eBay's enormous platform, you don't need to worry about marketing, SEO or paying for traffic. This saves you time, as marketing is one of the biggest challenges associated with launching a dropshipping business.

The Cons of Selling on eBay

Listing Fees – The biggest downside to eBay are the fees you'll have to pay. The most notable is the success fee, which can be up to 10% – or higher – of the sale prices of your items. In the dropshipping market, where margins are already fairly thin, this will cut into a large portion of your profits.

Constant Monitoring and Re-Listing – eBay is an auction-style marketplace, so you'll need to be constantly monitoring and re-listing the products you want to sell. Some tools help automate this process, but it's still not as straightforward as listing a static product for sale on your own ecommerce website.

Can't Customize Your Sales Platform – Your product listings need to follow eBay templates, making it more difficult to create a professional, value-adding page for your items.

No Long-Term Connection With Customers – You might have a few repeat eBay customers, but most will probably never buy from you again. Any goodwill you bank up through excellent service will likely be lost.

The marketplace structure is created to serve itself. eBay doesn't want to focus on the merchants (you), they only want to focus on the products. You will be significantly restricted in how you communicate with customers, how you brand yourself, the design of your store, and so on.

You're Not Building an Asset – When you create a store that generates traffic and has repeat customers, you're building a real business with value that you can sell to someone else. When you sell on eBay, you're not building a lasting brand or web property with any tangible value that can be sold in the future.

14. Dropshipping on Amazon

Although Amazon stocks and sells a number of items, many of the products listed are actually sold by third-party merchants via Amazon's website. Like eBay, Amazon acts to help facilitate the sale and to resolve any problems that arise.

The Pros of Selling on Amazon
The advantages of selling on Amazon are similar to the ones discussed for eBay: it's easy to get started, you have immediate access to a large audience and you don't need to worry about marketing or SEO.

Amazon also offers its own fulfillment warehouses (Fulfillment by Amazon), which allow you to complement your drop shipped items with products of your own without having to deal with packing, shipping or warehousing.

The Cons of Selling on Amazon

Listing Fees – As with eBay, you pay for access to this large network of buyers through fairly substantial commission fees. Amazon's commission fees vary by product type but are usually in the 10% to 15% range.

Again, if you're working with relatively small dropshipping margins, this will take a hefty chunk out of your profits.

Exposure of Sales Data – One risk you take using Amazon's platform is that Amazon can see all of your sales data, from the items that sell best to how much you're selling overall. Amazon has been accused of using this data to identify great selling opportunities and strengthen its own involvement in the niche, ultimately pushing out other merchants selling through its marketplace.

No Long-Term Connection With Customers – Same deal as eBay, it's unlikely that you'll be able to grow a long-term relationship with your customers. Amazon exists to help themselves, so it's in there best interest to focus on the products and not the sellers. Be prepared to be severely restricted on how you can brand your business, display your products and communicate with your customers.

No Customization – Again like eBay you're going to be really limited in terms of customization. Everything you do in terms of branding, UI, marketing, and everything else is under Amazon's control.

15. Dropshipping With Your Own Online Store

The alternative to selling through third-party sites like Amazon and eBay is establishing your own online store to sell products. This is the method that attracts most people interested in building a successful dropshipping business.

The Pros of Selling on Your Own Store

More Control – With your own online store you get to create a shopping environment that's conductive to selling your products and – most importantly – adding value to your customers. You can customize the look and layout, and create custom product pages optimized to best inform your customers about the products.

Easy Design – Building your own ecommerce store is easy, especially with platforms like Shopify. Simply choose a store design out of hundreds of options, make any customizations you want, add your products, hook up a payment gateway and you're up and running. Depending on the type of online store you're looking to create, you can be up and running in one day.

Mobile Ready – Selling on eBay and Amazon via mobile can be a pain. If you choose to build your online store with well respected hosted ecommerce platform your site will likely be responsive, which means it will look great on an iPad or mobile phone. This is increasingly important these days, as nearly 30% of online purchases are made via a mobile device.

Some online store platforms, like Shopify, let you manage your entire business from your mobile device. This is particularly attractive to dropshipping business owners who often like to run their business on-the-go, or even on the beach somewhere.

No Third-Party Fees – You won't have to pay 10% to 15% of every sale to eBay or Amazon, which will significantly improve your profit margins. All-in-all you're going to make more money by setting your dropshipping business up with an online store.

Building a Real Business – You're able to build a long-term business with a distinctive feel, known expertise and repeat customers. Most importantly, you'll be building a business with equity. It's much easier to sell a business built around an independently owned website.

The Cons of Selling on Your Own Store

Less Free Traffic – With your own site, you'll be responsible for generating traffic through marketing, SEO and paid advertising. There's more cost involved – either money or time invested – and you'll need to be willing to invest in a long-term campaign to promote your new store.

Increased Complexity – On Amazon and eBay, you don't have to think too much; simply fill out the standard template and publish your product listing. With your own site, you're ultimately responsible for configuring the design, layout and structure of your store. And if you're hosting your own store (versus using a hosted service like Shopify), you'll be responsible for any technical configuration related to the software and servers.

Which Sales Strategy Should You Choose?

So which platform should you choose? There's a lot to consider, and different platforms will be better suited for different people and situations.

If you're looking to dip your toes into the dropshipping waters and explore it as a hobby, selling on eBay and Amazon can be a viable way to move forward if you can find products with enough margin to cover your fees and still make a profit. There are many people making money selling on eBay and Amazon so you shouldn't dismiss it.

But if you're serious about building a long-term business, we recommend starting your own ecommerce store. As discussed above, it offers the most flexibility, customization, ability to connect with customers, the chance to build real brand equity, and so much more. You'll need to invest in marketing and promotion, especially in the early days, but we think it offers the best long-term potential and is truly the only option for those serious about selling online.

Also, there's nothing wrong with selling a few items on eBay and Amazon while you're in the early stages of building your store. In fact, a number of mature, established brands sell merchandise this way, particularly through Amazon.

16. Running a Dropshipping Company

If you've never run a dropshipping business, the information in this chapter could save you weeks of wasted time and frustration. Many of these detailed suggestions are drawn from two basic principles about dropshipping:

1. Accept That Things Can Get Messy – The convenience of dropshipping comes at a price, and having an invisible third party involved in each sale often complicates things. From botched orders to out-of-stock items, fulfillment problems will be something you'll have to deal with. If you accept this ahead of time, you're less likely to throw in the towel due to frustration.

2. Adopt a KISS Mentality – Having a KISS (Keep It Simple, Stupid!) mentality will serve you well with the dropshipping model. Given the inherent complexity of dropshipping – multiple suppliers, shipments from various locations, etc. – it's easy to think you need to set your system to perfectly track your costs and inventory at all times. But if you try to do this, you'll likely go crazy, spend thousands on custom development and never launch a store. Focusing on the easiest-to-implement solutions, even if they're not "perfect," is usually the better option – especially when you're starting out.

With these two concepts in mind, let's discuss how to structure your business operationally to make things run as smoothly as possible.

When Suppliers Botch an Order

Even great suppliers make mistakes, and you're guaranteed to have fulfillment errors from time to time. So what do you do when your supplier sends the wrong item – or nothing at all?

Own the Mistake – Under no circumstances should you blame your dropshipper for the mistake. It will only cause confusion and make you look like an amateur. The customer has no idea the drop shipper even exists. Instead, you need to own the problem, apologize and let the customer know what you're doing to fix it.

Make It Up to Them – Depending on the level of the mistake, you may want to proactively offer the customer something for the error. This could mean refunding the shipping fee (a personal favorite of ours) or an upgrade if the customer needs a new item shipped out.

Make the Supplier Pay to Fix It – You may have to assume responsibility for the error, but that doesn't mean you need to pay for it! Any reputable supplier will pay to fix its own errors, including paying for shipping costs to return items. However, it probably won't pay for any freebies or upgrades you gave the customer (see above). You need to chalk those up as public relations and brand-building expenses.

Again, even the best suppliers will occasionally make mistakes, but be extremely wary of a supplier that habitually botches your orders and fails to fulfill them properly. Unless you can get the supplier to change (unlikely), your business's reputation will suffer. If this is the case, you should probably start looking for another supplier.

17. Managing Inventory & Suppliers

Most experienced dropshippers would agree that managing the status of inventory across multiple suppliers is the biggest challenge you'll face running a dropshipping business. Do a poor job of this and you'll be constantly informing customers that their order is out of stock – not a great way to attract repeat business and loyal brand fans.

Properly managing inventory across your suppliers – and limiting the number of out-of-stock items you sell – is a complex process. Web-based services, like Ordoro and eCommHub can help you sync inventory. This is a great option when suppliers offer real-time data feeds, but suppliers don't always have them.

Below are some best practices for inventory management that should help drastically reduce the number of out-of-stock items you sell:

Use Multiple Suppliers – Having access to multiple suppliers can be a huge advantage. Why? Because having multiple suppliers with overlapping inventory is the BEST way to improve your order fulfillment ratio. If supplier A doesn't have an item in stock, there's a good chance supplier B has it. Additionally, it's risky to rely on one supplier as the only place to source your product. If they decide not to work with you, raise their prices or go out of business it jeopardizes the future of your business.

You'll never be able to find two suppliers that carry all the same products, but if they operate in the same niche or industry, both will likely stock the best-selling items – and these are what you're most concerned about.

Pick Your Products Wisely – Drawing on the last point, try to sell primarily items that you know are carried by both suppliers. This way, you have two potential fulfillment options.

Use Generics to Your Advantage – Even if they don't have exactly the same item, two suppliers might carry near-identical products that are interchangeable. This is particularly true for smaller accessories and product add-ons. If you can confirm that two products are nearly identical, write a generic product description that allows you to fulfill the order from either supplier. Also, list both suppliers' model numbers in the model field. That way you can forward an order invoice to either supplier without having to make changes.

A word of warning: You need to exercise some judgment in this area. Each market will have well-known brands (e.g., Nike, Bose), and you should NEVER substitute those products.

Check on Item Availability – Just because a dropshipper lists an item on its website doesn't mean it carries that item consistently. It's a good idea to chat with your sales representative about the availability of products you're considering selling. Are these items in stock 90% of the time or more? Or does the dropshipper keep only a few on hand and often has trouble getting the product reordered from the manufacturer? You'll want to avoid stocking the latter type of products.

Dealing With Out-of-Stock Orders - Despite your best planning, you'll inevitably deal with customer orders you can't fill. Instead of telling the customer the item is out of stock, offer a complimentary upgrade to a similar – but better – product. Your customer will likely be thrilled, and you'll be able to retain the customer relationship. You might not make any money on the order, and that's OK. You wouldn't have made any money had your customer canceled the order, either.

Order Fulfillment

Utilizing multiple suppliers has a number of benefits that we've discussed: it increases the likelihood that items will be in stock, offers geographical diversity for faster delivery times and prevents you from being reliant on any one source for your products. But with multiple options for filling an order, how do you know which supplier to choose? There are a few different methods to consider:

Route All Orders to a Preferred Supplier – If you have one supplier that's best to work with (superior service, great selection, etc.), you can simply route all orders to that supplier by default. This is particularly easy to implement, as you can simply add your supplier's email address as a recipient for all new order confirmations, automating the entire process. If you use this method, ideally your preferred supplier will stock most of the items you sell. Otherwise, you'll frequently have to deal with re-routing orders that it couldn't fill.

Route Orders Based on Location – If you use multiple suppliers that each stock the majority of your products, you can simply route the order to the supplier closest to your customer. This not only expedites delivery to your customer, but also saves on shipping fees.

Route Orders Based on Availability – If you stock a large catalog of products spread out over numerous suppliers, you'll likely need to route each order based on which drop shipper has the item in stock. This option requires more work if you're doing it manually but can be automated with a service like eCommHub (www.ecommhub.com) if your suppliers provide data feeds.

Route Orders Based on Price – This sounds great in theory, but unless one supplier has significantly better pricing it can be difficult to automatically determine which supplier will be cheapest. Any automated solution will need to consider potential drop fees, real-time shipping rates and real-time supplier pricing. So while not impossible, it can be difficult to implement an accurate automated system to accomplish this.

Note: Even if you don't route all your orders on price, you should have your suppliers bid against each other to achieve the best pricing possible as your business grows. Just don't try to do this too early – if you're asking for pricing discounts as a newbie, you'll likely only annoy your suppliers.

We've tried all four methods and found there's no "best" way to do it. It really depends on your store, your suppliers and your personal preferences.

Security and Fraud Issues

Storing Credit Card Numbers
Storing your customers' credit card information can allow for convenient reordering and may increase sales. But if you're hosting your own site, this typically isn't worth the security issues and liability. To store credit card data you'll need to abide by all sorts of PCI (Payment Card Industry) compliance rules and security audits. This process is expensive and complex, especially for non-technical merchants. And if your server is hacked or breached, you might be liable for the stolen card information.

The best solution is to not store your customers' credit card data. Focus your efforts on marketing and customer service instead of security audits. Fortunately, if you're using a hosted platform like Shopify you won't need to worry about any of this. But if you're using a self-hosted cart, make sure to disable the "store card information" feature in your configuration panel.

Dealing With Fraudulent Orders
The possibility of fraudulent orders can be scary when you're starting out, but with some common sense and a bit of caution you can prevent the vast majority of losses due to fraud.

The Address Verification System
The most common and widely used fraud prevention measure is the AVS, or address verification system. When the AVS feature is enabled, customers must enter the address on file with their credit card for the transaction to be approved. This helps prevent thieves with just the raw credit card number from successfully making purchases online. Fraud is rare for orders that pass the AVS check and are shipped to the customers' billing addresses.

The vast majority of fraudulent ecommerce orders occur when the billing and shipping addresses are different. In these cases, a thief enters the card owner's address as the billing address and enters a separate shipping address for the goods. Unfortunately, if you don't allow customers to ship to addresses other than the billing address, you'll lose out on a lot of legitimate orders. But by allowing it, you're at risk for fraudulent orders that YOU will have to pay for. If you ship an order to an address other than the card holder's address, the credit card company will make you foot the bill in the event of fraud.

Fortunately, fraudsters tend to follow patterns that make it easier to spot illegitimate orders before they ship. Individually, these signs won't help you flag a fraudulent order, but if you see two or three of them you should investigate:

Different Billing and Shipping – Again, more than 95% of all fraudulent orders will have different billing and shipping addresses.

Different Names – Different names on the billing and shipping addresses could be a red flag for fraudulent orders. That, or a gift purchase.

Unusual Email Addresses – Most people have email addresses incorporating some part of their name, allowing you to match part of an email address to a customer's name. But if you see an address like dfssdfsdf@gmail.com, there's a good chance it's a made-up address and is one sign of fraud.

Expedited Shipping – Since they're charging everything to someone else's card, fraudsters will often pick the fastest – and most expensive – delivery method. It also reduces the amount of time you have to catch them before the item is delivered.
If you spot an order you suspect is fraudulent, simply pick up the phone. Fraudsters almost never put their real number on an order. If the order is legitimate, you'll likely have a 30-second discussion with someone that clears everything up. If not, you'll get a dead number or someone who has no idea that she ordered a 25-foot boat

scheduled for overnight delivery. At that point, you can cancel the order and issue a refund to avoid any chargebacks or problems.

Understanding Chargebacks

When a customer calls his or her bank or credit card company to contest a charge made by you, you'll receive what's called a "chargeback." Your payment processor will temporarily deduct the amount of the disputed charge from your account and ask you to prove that you delivered the goods or services to the customer. If you can't provide proof, you'll lose the amount in question and be slapped with a $25 chargeback processing fee. If you rack up too many chargebacks relative to the volume of orders you're processing, you could even lose your merchant account.

The largest cause of chargebacks is usually fraud, but customers will also dispute a charge because they didn't recognize your business, forgot about the transaction or simply didn't like the product they received. We've seen it all.

When you receive a chargeback, you often have just a few days to respond, so you need to act quickly! To have a shot at getting your money back, you'll need to provide documentation of the original order, tracking information showing delivery and likely a wholesale packing slip showing which items you purchased and shipped. If the contested charge was for a legitimate transaction, you'll have a good chance of recovering the funds as long as you didn't make any untrue statements or promises in the course of the transaction.

Unfortunately, if the chargeback is related to an order with different billing and shipping addresses, you're almost certainly not going to win. Most processors will only compensate you for fraudulent orders shipped to the billing address on the card. In our businesses, we don't even bother responding to these kind of chargebacks because we know it's a waste of time.

Dealing With Returns

Before writing your own return policy, you'll want to make sure you know and understand how all your suppliers deal with returns. If they have a lax 45-day return window, you can afford to be generous with your terms. A strict return policy from just one supplier can cause you to re-evaluate the terms you can afford to have in place.

When a customer needs to return an item, the process will look like this:

A customer contacts you to request a return
You request an RMA (return merchandise authorization) number from your supplier
The customer mails back the merchandise to your supplier, noting the RMA # on the address
The supplier refunds your account for the wholesale price of the merchandise
You refund the customer for the full price of the merchandise
It's not always this straightforward, however. The following can complicate returns:

Restocking Fees
Some suppliers will charge a restocking fee, which is essentially a surcharge for having to return an item. Even if your supplier charges these fees, we strongly recommend not having them be a part of your return policy. They seem outdated and unfriendly toward customers. Although you may have to eat a fee here and there, you'll likely recoup that expense in more customers who decide to do business with you.

Defective Items
The only thing worse than receiving a defective item is having to pay additional postage to return it! Most dropshipping suppliers won't cover return postage for defective items. In their minds, they didn't manufacture the item so they aren't liable for defects. They simply view it as a risk of selling products to a retail market.

You, however, should ALWAYS compensate your customers for the return shipping fees for defective items if you're interested in building a reputable business. Again, this is a fee you won't be able to pass along to anyone, but it's part of the cost of running a quality dropshipping business. Unless you have your own UPS or FedEx account, it can be difficult to print a pre-paid shipping label for customers so you may need to issue a return shipping refund to compensate them for their out-of-pocket expense. However you do it, make sure you compensate them somehow.

If the defective item is relatively inexpensive, it often makes sense to just ship the customer a new product without requiring them to return the old one. This has a number of advantages compared to making them return the old item, including:

It Can Be Cost Effective – It doesn't make sense to pay $10 to return an item that only costs you $12 from your wholesaler. You'll get a $2 net credit, but it's not worth it for the hassle to your customer, supplier and staff.

The Customer Is Blown Away – How often do companies simply ship out a new product without needing an old one back? Almost never! You'll score major points and may land a customer for life. Also, the customer will get the new product much faster than if the old one had to be returned to the warehouse before the new item could be shipped.

Your Supplier May Pay for Shipping – Suppliers won't pay for return shipping on a defective product, but most will pay to have a new replacement sent to the customer. Because they'll be paying for return shipping anyway, most suppliers can be talked into covering the shipping on a replacement product that you simply purchase separately. Plus, many are glad to duck the hassle of processing the return.

If a customer wants to return a non-defective product for a refund, most companies will expect the buyer to pay for the return freight. This is a fairly reasonable policy. If you're willing to offer free returns on everything, you'll definitely stand out (and companies like Zappos have made this part of their unique business model). But it can get expensive, and most customers will understand that you shouldn't have to cough up return shipping fees simply because they ordered a product they ultimately didn't want.

18. Shipping Issues

Calculating shipping rates can be a big mess for dropshipping merchants. With so many different products shipping from multiple locations, it's difficult to accurately calculate shipping rates for orders.

There are three types of shipping rates you can use:

Real-Time Rates – With this method, your shopping cart will use the collective weight of all items purchased and the shipping destination to get an actual real-time quote. This is very accurate but can be difficult to compute for shipments from multiple warehouses.

Per-Type Rates – Using a per-type method, you'll set flat shipping rates based on the types of products ordered. So all small widgets would ship for a flat $5 rate, while all large widgets would be $10 to ship.

Flat-Rate Shipping – As the name implies, you'd charge one flat rate for all shipments, regardless of type. You could even offer free shipping on all orders. This method is the easiest to implement but is the least accurate in reflecting actual shipping costs.

When it comes to shipping, it's important to refer to the overarching principles about dropshipping that we listed at the outset of this chapter. Specifically, we want to find a solution that emphasizes simplicity over perfection, especially if we're just starting out.

Some merchants will spend days – or weeks – struggling to properly configure automated shipping rules for a store that has yet to generate a sale. Instead, they should focus on other issues like marketing and customer service, and quickly implement a shipping policy that makes sense from an overall level. Then, once they start to grow, they can invest in a more exact system. With this philosophy, it's often best to estimate an average shipping fee and set that as your overall flat rate. You'll probably lose money on some orders but make it back on others.

Even if you could implement a system that passed along extra shipping fees based on supplier location, would you really want to? Most customers balk at excessive shipping fees, especially when they assume their order is originating from one location. Instead, try to limit multiple shipments by using suppliers with overlapping inventory and by being selective about the items you sell. This is a much more practical and simple long-term solution.

International Shipments
International shipping has become easier but it's still not as straightforward as domestic shipping. When you ship internationally, you'll need to consider and/or deal with:

Different weight and length limitations for different countries
Additional charges from suppliers for processing international orders
The added expense of resolving problematic orders due to higher shipping fees
Excessive costs for shipping large and/or heavy items
Is the hassle worth it? It depends on the market you're in and the margins you earn. If you sell small items with higher margins, the increased market reach may make it worthwhile to deal with the hassle and expense of offering international shipments. For others –

especially merchants selling larger or heavier items – the added benefit won't be worth the expense and inconvenience.

Picking a Carrier
Selecting the right carrier is important, as it can save you a significant amount of money. In the U.S., the largest decision you'll need to make is between UPS/FedEx and the U.S. Postal Service.

UPS/FedEx – These privately run giants are great for shipping large, heavy packages domestically. Their rates for big shipments will be significantly lower than those charged by the USPS.

U.S. Postal Service – If you're shipping small, lightweight items you can't beat the rates offered by the USPS. After dropshipping fees, the cheapest UPS shipping fee you're likely to see is around $10, while you can often ship items for $5 or less through the post office.

The post office tends to be a better choice for sending international shipments, especially smaller ones.

When setting up your shipping options, consider categorizing them by shipping time ("Within 5 Days" or "Within 3 Days"), as this gives you the flexibility to pick the carrier that's the most economical for each order and delivery time.

19. Providing Customer Support

Take it from us: Managing all your customer emails, requests and returns in an Excel spreadsheet is NOT ideal. As excellent as Excel is, it's not built to handle customer support. Similarly, as your business and team grow, managing support with a single email inbox also quickly breaks down and leads to problems and service lapses.

Implementing a help desk is one of the best things you can do to ensure quality service for your customers. Help desk software comes in a number of different forms, but all provide a centralized location to manage your customer support correspondence and issues. Most desks make it easy to assign issues to team members and maintain communication history among all related parties.

A few popular options to choose from include:

Help Scout – Less cluttered than other desks, Help Scout treats each issue as an email and removes all the traditionally appended ticket information that customers see with support requests. Instead, support tickets appear like standard emails to customers, creating a more personalized experience.

Zendesk – Highly customizable and powerful, Zendesk offers a variety of tools and integrations and is one of the most popular help desks available. It takes some customization but is very powerful once it's tailored to your company.

Desk – Backed by well-known SalesForce, Desk's 'Universal Inbox' allows you to interact with your customers across numerous channels from one streamlined interface.

Kayako – Kayako boasts an all-in-one platform that offers built-in live chat, phone call and remote support issue management alongside traditional ticket-based support.

Offering Phone Support

Deciding whether to offer phone support can be a tricky decision. It's obviously a great way to provide real-time support but is one of the most expensive support methods. If you're bootstrapping a business while working your 9 to 5, you won't be able to handle calls. But if you're working full-time on your business – or have a staff member who can – it might be a feasible option. If you're unable to staff a phone throughout the day, you can always have your phone number ring through to voicemail and return customer calls later. This isn't a perfect solution but can be a good compromise.

You should consider the type of products you'll be selling when thinking about how to offer phone support. If you're a diamond boutique selling jewelry in the $1,000 to $5,000 range, many customers won't be comfortable placing an order that large without talking to a real person. However, if you're selling products in the $25 to $50 range, most people will feel comfortable buying without phone support, assuming you've built a professional, information-rich website.

If you do decide to offer phone support, think through strategic ways to do so. Slapping a large 800 number on the top of every page can lead to a surfeit of low-value phone calls that cost more to support than they're worth. Instead, consider adding your number in more strategic places like the Contact Us and Shopping Cart pages, where you know the visitor has a high probability of purchasing.

Regardless of how you decide to handle sales requests, you should always be willing to call customers after the sale to resolve any issues that arise. There's nothing wrong with carefully evaluating the best ways to offer pre-sale support, but when it comes to taking care of people who have purchased from you, you should never refuse to help them on the phone.

The following services can help you set up a toll-free number and sales line:

Grasshopper – Grasshopper offers phone services and is geared toward smaller businesses and entrepreneurs. You can get a toll-free number, unlimited extensions, call forwarding and voicemail for a reasonable monthly fee (around $25).

RingCentral – RingCentral is the 800-pound gorilla in the VoIP and 800-number space, and we've used it in the past with mixed results. Its flexible interface lets you set up custom routing rules and extensions. For Mac users, we recommend looking for a different company unless you plan on buying a VoIP phone, as RingCentral's phone software for OS X is buggy and unreliable.

20. The Key Elements of Success

We've covered a bunch of information so far, discussing everything from the fundamentals of dropshipping to the intricacies of picking a niche and running your business. By now, you should have enough of a foundation to confidently get started researching and launching your own dropshipping business.

With so much to consider, it's easy to get overwhelmed and lose track of what's really important. That's why we created this list of the crucial elements to success. These are the core "must-do" actions that will make or break your new venture. If you can successfully execute these, you'll be able to get a lot of other things wrong and still have a great chance at success.

1. Add Value

Having a solid plan for how you can add value to your customers is the most crucial success factor. This is important for all businesses, but much more so in the world of dropshipping, where you'll be competing with legions of other "me too" shops carrying similar products.

With dropshipping, it's easy to think you're selling customers a product. But successful small merchants understand that it's not only the product they offer – they're selling insights, information and solutions. You think you're an ecommerce merchant but you're also in the information business.

So how are you going to add value and help solve problems for your customers? If you're unsure, spend some time re-reading Chapter 4, which discusses the topic in depth. If you're struggling to answer this question for a given niche, you may want to consider picking a different market.

If you're not able to add value through quality information and guidance, the only thing you're left to compete on is price. While this has been a successful strategy for Walmart, it's not going to help you build a successful drop shipping business.

2. Focus on Marketing and SEO

Coming in a close second to adding value as a key success factor is being able to drive traffic to your new site. The #1 problem and frustration new ecommerce merchants face is a lack of traffic to their websites. Too many merchants slave away for months on the perfect site only to launch it to a world that has no idea it exists.

Marketing and driving traffic is absolutely essential to the success of your business and is difficult to outsource well, especially if you have a small budget and are bootstrapping your business. You need to take the personal initiative to develop your own SEO, marketing, outreach and guest posting skills.

This is particularly crucial during the first 6 to 12 months, when no one knows who you are. Following your site launch, you need to dedicate at least 75% of your time on marketing, SEO and traffic generation for at least 4 to 6 months – that's right, 4 to 6 months! Once you've established a solid marketing foundation, you can scale back and coast a bit on the work you put in. But early on, it's impossible to place too much emphasis on marketing.

If you're not a marketing or SEO expert yet, the following resources and blogs are a great way to get started:

SEO Resources:

SEOmoz – One of the most popular SEO communities online. Their beginners guide to SEO is a particularly great resource for those starting out.

SeachEngineLand – Extremely prolific SEO blog, with dozens of new posts each day.

SEOBook – A popular SEO blog and the home of a paid private community for SEO professionals.

Distilled – This marketing and SEO agency has a top-notch blog and a number of quality training courses and guides, many of which are free.

Marketing Resources:
Hubspot Blog – Advice on everything inbound marketing related, from driving traffic with email to social media tips.

Seth Godin's Blog – Solid high-level advice on marketing and building an audience.

QuickSprout – A blog by well-known entrepreneur Neil Patel dedicated largely to marketing, SEO and traffic generation.

KissMetrics Blog – In-depth marketing posts with a slant toward analytics, usability and conversion.

SparringMind – How to use behavioral psychology to help influence customers and market your business.

CopyBlogger – Content marketing tips with an emphasis on writing effective, compelling copywriting.

Mixergy – Interviews with successful entrepreneurs in the technology and online fields. Not focused exclusively on marketing, but lots of applicable information for aspiring entrepreneurs including marketing and early-stage advice.

Ecommerce Marketing Resources:
Shopify Blog – A comprehensive ecommerce blog with frequent posts on how to effectively promote and market your online store.

3. Specialize!

Almost every successful dropshipping store we encounter has one thing in common: It specializes in a certain product or niche. The more that stores specialize, the more successful they tend to be.

You don't want to just sell backpacks. You want to sell backpacks designed for around-the-world travelers obsessed with lightweight gear. You don't want to just sell security camera equipment. You want to focus on security systems for gas stations.

Many think narrowing their focus limits their potential customer base and will cost them sales. Just the opposite is true! Specializing allows you to communicate more effectively with your customers, stand out more easily from the competition and compete against a smaller field. Specializing is rarely a bad move to make in a dropshipping venture.

If you're launching a store in a new niche you probably won't know what segment of your customers to focus on – and that's OK. But as you gain experience with your customers you should identify the segment that's the most profitable and that allows you to add the most value. Then, try to position your business to focus exclusively on those customers' needs and problems. You'll be amazed at how your conversion rates skyrocket even if you're charging a premium price.

Remember: If everyone is your customer, then no one is. Specialization makes it easier to differentiate yourself, charge a premium price and concentrate your marketing efforts more effectively.

4. Have a Long-Term Perspective

Building a dropshipping business is like building anything else of value: It takes a significant level of commitment and investment over time. Yet for some reason people assume they can build a passive six-figure income with dropshipping after a few months of part-time work. That's just not the way it works.

As we mentioned in Chapter 5, it will realistically take at least a year to build a business that generates an average full-time income.

It's also important to understand that the first few months are the most difficult. You'll struggle with doubts, run into issues with your website and will likely have an underwhelming website launch that generates zero sales. Understand that this is normal! Rome wasn't built in a day, and neither were any successful dropshipping businesses.

If you mentally prepare for a challenging beginning and don't expect to get rich overnight, you'll be much more likely to stick with your business until it becomes a success.

5. Offer Outstanding Service

The Internet has always been a fairly transparent place, but the recent rise of social media has made your business reputation even more important to your success online. If you don't treat your customers well, they'll often let the entire world know – including many potential customers.

The biggest customer service risk for dropshipping merchants is having tunnel vision on per-order profits and losses when fulfillment issues go awry. As discussed in Chapter 6, it's critical to accept that dropshipping can get messy, that you'll be paying to clean up some messes, and that you shouldn't always try to pass these on to your customer. If you aren't occasionally losing money on individual orders to make customers happy, you're probably not providing very good service.

Having happy customers is some of – if not THE – best marketing you can do. As is true in all businesses, it's much easier to make a sale to a satisfied customer than to try to convince a new prospect to buy. If you treat your customers exceptionally well, they're likely to spread the word and refer others your way. With top-notch service, you can build a business where repeat customers generate much of your revenue.

Making customer service a priority set your dropshipping business up for success, so ensure it's a priority from the outset.

6. Don't Get Hung Up on the Details

Don't focus too much on the details. Your company name, logo, theme or email marketing service aren't going to determine your success.

What makes a business successful are the things we just talked about: adding value, marketing, outstanding customer service, specializing and a long-term commitment. Still, new merchants will spend weeks – sometimes months – struggling to make a decision between two shopping carts or providers. That's valuable time better spent developing the core aspects of the business.

Do your research and make an informed decision, but don't let small decisions paralyze you.

7. The Most Important Step

The most important step – the one that most people never take – is to actually get started building your business! This is the hardest thing for most people and it's usually a result of fear and uncertainty.

It's a common misconception that successful entrepreneurs have a rock-solid certainty about their business at the outset. When you dig a little deeper, you'll find that most had fears and reservations about how things would turn out. Yet they moved forward with their plan despite these doubts.

If you're serious about building your own dropshipping business, you'll need to do the same. Do your research, evaluate your options and then move forward with that information in spite of your fears and reservations. It's what entrepreneurs do. Start now.

21. THANK YOU FOR READING!

Thank You so much for reading this book. If this title gave you a ton of value, It would be amazing for you to leave a <u>REVIEW</u> !

<u>THANK YOU FOR DOWNLOADING! IF YOU WOULD LIKE TO BECOME APART OF OUR READER COMMUNITY AND RECEIVE UPDATES ON UPCOMING TITLES PLEASE EMAIL PARAMOUNTPUBLISHINGCO@ GMAIL.COM</u>